San Francisco Shake-Up

Jocelyn Sigue

Illustrated by Béatrice Lebreton

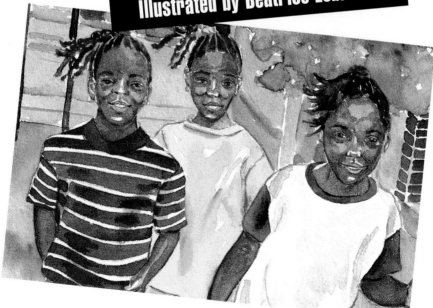

Rigby

© 1997 by Rigby,
a division of Reed Elsevier Inc.
500 Coventry Lane
Crystal Lake, IL 60014

03 02 01
10 9 8 7 6 5 4

Printed in Singapore

ISBN 0-7635-3228-2

"You have to make sure your batteries work," I explained to Keesha and Cherie while I changed the batteries in my two flashlights. "That's what we learned in the earthquake drill at school that day."

"We have a flashlight," they sang together.

"But are the batteries working?" I asked.

"Sure... they must be," they answered. "Let's go outside, Raven!"

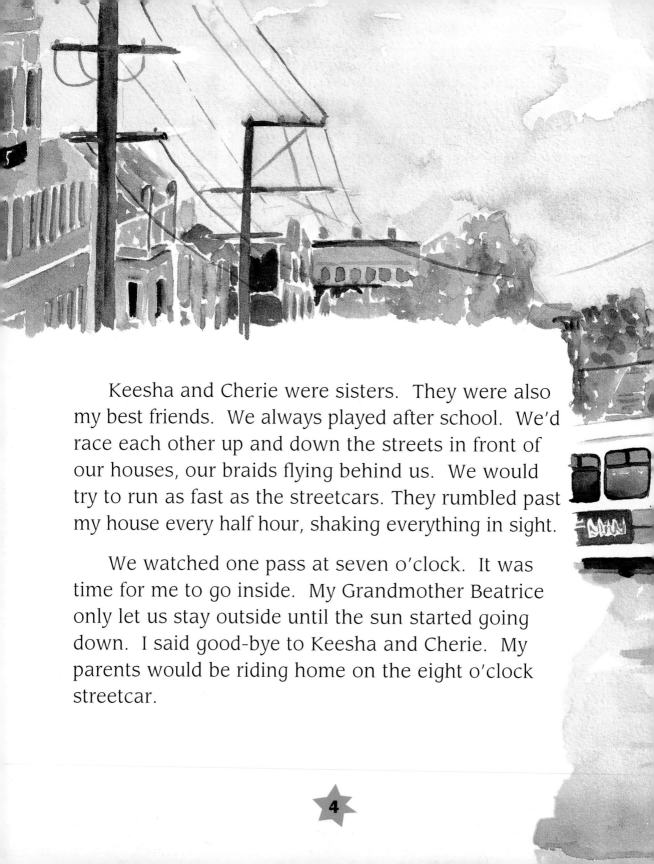

Keesha and Cherie were sisters. They were also my best friends. We always played after school. We'd race each other up and down the streets in front of our houses, our braids flying behind us. We would try to run as fast as the streetcars. They rumbled past my house every half hour, shaking everything in sight.

We watched one pass at seven o'clock. It was time for me to go inside. My Grandmother Beatrice only let us stay outside until the sun started going down. I said good-bye to Keesha and Cherie. My parents would be riding home on the eight o'clock streetcar.

Grandmother Bea told me stories while we waited for my parents to come home from work. A lot of her stories were about Africa, where our family had come from years ago. Her favorite story was about the masks she brought back to America from Mali, a small country in western Africa.

The masks were hanging in the living room. She told me that fierce warriors once had worn them. I imagined what it was like to be fierce.

My grandmother let me play with one of the masks. I lost my balance and fell in the middle of my act as an African warrior. My grandmother and I laughed at my clumsiness.

We shouldn't have laughed. I had fallen because the house was shaking.

The rumbling streetcar passes by only once every half hour, I thought. When I looked at the clock, it read 7:15. At first I sat in amazement. I watched my grandmother's chair vibrate. The lamp next to her bounced around on its table.

Then it hit me... EARTHQUAKE!!!

"Grandmother Bea, get under the table!" I screamed as I crawled. I remembered that day's drill in school: Get under something sturdy because things could start falling.

But Grandmother Bea pointed to her bad knee. It would hurt if she crawled.

"Go to the doorway, Grandmother Bea," I told her. "You'll be safe there." Doorways are where people who can't get under a table should hide during earthquakes.

The living room looked like a light show. The lights above me flew around like dizzy birds. The table lamps tipped from side to side. My grandmother's old family pictures on the wall were swinging.

So was the one mask I hadn't taken from the wall. I had to save it before it fell. Right hand, left leg, left hand, right leg, I slowly crawled out from under the table.

CRASH! The lamp fell from the table and smashed to the floor. Just then, it seemed like everything in the room was falling. I heard the tinkle of glass breaking and the clank of wooden chairs hitting the floor. I had no choice but to back up, left leg, right hand, right leg, left hand. I watched the mask the whole time. It was dancing on the wall.

Suddenly everything stopped. Phew! The mask hadn't fallen.

"Grandmother Bea, are you okay?" I asked.

She was still standing in the doorway. "Yes, Raven."

"Don't move," I told her. "After earthquakes we have… AFTERSHOCKS! And here they come!"

The aftershock lasted only a few seconds. That was just long enough for the second mask to fly off of the wall. I reached out, trying to catch it. But the mask had disappeared.

Everything had disappeared because I couldn't see a thing. The lights were out. A glance out the window told me that all of the lights on the block were out. The earthquake was over.

"Raven? Where are you, dear?" I could hear my grandmother moving closer to me, but I couldn't see her.

"Here, Grandmother Bea."

"Are you okay?" she asked me.

"Yes, but I think your mask is broken. We have to find it." I stumbled out from under the table.

"No, don't worry about it," she said, grabbing my hand.

"But, Grandmother Bea, it's your favorite."

"We need to see how everyone in the neighborhood is first. Then we will worry about the things we can replace," she told me while pulling me outside.

"Wait, Grandmother Bea," I said. I made my way to the kitchen, where I had left the flashlights.

Outside the whole block was quiet. Grandmother Bea and I panned the area with our tiny spotlights. Our neighbors were outside. Their mouths were hanging open. The streets didn't look the same. The sidewalks were lined with fallen telephone poles. The quake had shaken them right out of the ground. No one would be using the phone for a while. Luckily the streetcar wires hadn't fallen. Still, no streetcars would be passing by. They ran on electricity, and the electricity was out. With no streetcars running, my parents would be stuck somewhere.

I realized then why it was so quiet. I didn't see or even hear Keesha and Cherie. If I made it outside, they should have also.

"Grandmother Bea, we have to see if my friends are okay." I grabbed her hand and pulled her next door to their house.

"Keesha, Cherie… Mr. and Mrs. Williams?" I shouted at the front window as I shined my light inside.

The house looked the same from the outside, but the inside was a completely different story. The living room looked like it had been flipped upside down. Things that were normally on one side of the room were now on the other side. I wondered if the rest of the house looked like this.

"Raven, is that you?" Mrs. Williams called back to me. "We're in the back, in Keesha and Cherie's room," she said.

I ran to their window and peaked inside. Things looked worse in there. The beds that were normally against the sides of the room were both in the middle. Keesha and Cherie's two wooden desks were lying on their sides. All of their books were on the floor.

The window to the room was open just enough for me to crawl inside and help them get out. I took a deep breath, and Grandmother Bea gave me a boost through the opening. Just then, I remembered one more step in the earthquake drill that I had forgotten. The gas needed to be shut off just in case there was a leak.

"Grandmother, we need to turn off the gas in our house," I told her. "Go home, I'll be safe here."

I shined my flashlight into the room. Keesha and Cherie and their parents were huddled between the two beds in the center of the mess of broken furniture, books, and toys.

"Thank goodness, Raven," Mr. Williams said. "The earthquake had us so shaken we couldn't tell right from left without the light."

I handed him the flashlight. He shut off their gas, then guided us all out of the front door.

"Getting out was so simple, but it didn't seem that way without a flashlight," Mr. Williams said, handing me back my flashlight. "The batteries are dead in ours. I guess none of us expected there would be an earthquake today. Right, girls?" He looked at Keesha and Cherie.

They shook their heads. I think they felt guilty for not listening to me.

"I guess you can never know when they're coming," I said. "I better go and check on my grandmother." I waved good-bye.

Grandmother Bea was in the big chair in the living room when I got home. Both African masks were sitting in pieces at her feet.

"I'm sorry, Grandmother Bea," I said. "I tried to save them."

"You couldn't save everyone and everything," she said.

"Will you tell me a story about the masks again, Grandmother Bea?" I asked.

She smiled and began her story as we waited for the electricity to come back on and the house to start rumbling again. This time, the rumbling would mean that the streetcar was finally bringing my parents home.